Kansas City BBQ

The How To and Where To of Kansas City Barbecue

BILL VENABLE III

PIG OUT PUBLICATIONS

Pig Out Publications
P.O. Box 14406
Kansas City, MO 64152

Printed in the United States of America

Contents

Acknowledgments   5

Introduction   7

The "How To" of Kansas City Barbecue   9

Paul Kirk, C.E.C.   13
    Barbecued Whole Hog   14
    Barbecued Pork Burgers   15
    The Baron's Barbecue Chicken   15
    Barbecued Rib Roast   16
    The Baron's Steak Sauce   16

Guy Simpson   17
    Guy's Chicken Wings   18
    Chinese Pork Loin   18
    Quick Grilled Pork Steaks   19
    Trout in a Basket   19
    Spicy Eye of Round Steak   20
    Fuzzy Navel Steak   20
    "Poor Man" Steak   21

Karen Putman, C.E.C.   23
    Smoked Chicken Salad   24
    Smoked Sausage Stuffed Duck   24
    Marinated Smoked Flank Steak   25
    Smoked Stuffed Veal   25
    Smoked Stuffed Leg of Lamb   26

Dan Morey   27
    Chef Dan's Leg of Lamb   28
    Smoked Brisket, K.C. Style   28
    Perfect Wild Game   29

Rich Davis   31
    Barbequed Whole Tenderloin   32
    K.C. Masterpiece Barbequed Baked Beans   32
    Barbecued Stuffed Cabbage Rolls   33
    Coleslaw with Boiled Dressing   34

Contents

Hasty-Bake   *35*
    Chad's "Baby Back" Ribs   37
    Simmons's Smoked Salmon   37
    Scott's S-m-o-o-t-h Orange Roughy   38
    Deb's Lip-Lickin' Chicken   38

The "Where To" of Kansas City Barbecue   *39*

Sample Survey   *40*

Results of Venable's 1989 Barbecue Survey   *41*
    Best Ribs in Town   41
    Best Beef in Town   41
    Best Ham in Town   41
    Best Chicken in Town   41
    Best Sauce in Town   42
    Best Beans in Town   42
    The Top BBQs in Town   42

Directory of Barbecue Restaurants   *43*

Books on Barbecue   *46*

Acknowledgments

Thoughts of an old tune on the radio ring in one's mind when philosophizing over the best tasting barbecue in Kansas City — "Any place where I hang my hat . . . is the place that I call home." So true it is with barbecue from our town. The "best tasting" award goes to the bones on your plate, the sauce on your lips, and the savory flavor on your tongue from your most recent barbecue meal.

Many friends have helped to make this book a reality; our survey took long hard hours to solicit and compile. Despite all efforts to remain unbiased, we still came up with the same answer: there are as many good places for barbecue as there are people to pick them. The barbecue restaurants listed here are the top twelve most mentioned in our survey of hundreds of Kansas City friends, neighbors, notables, and visitors. To all of you, many thanks.

Thanks also go to Jane Guthrie, without whose editorial expertise this book would have remained a pile of ramblings on magnetic tape. Her advice and counsel have made this book as hot as a mesquite coal.

Most of the recipes in this book come from my friends in the Kansas City Barbeque Society, a group I have learned many secrets from. Thanks for your input. My thanks also go to the members of the K.C. Bidnessmen team: Brad, Geary, Rick, Dr. Daniel, Wags, Riley Dog, Hogie and the Bass Weejun, and Ron and Dave and all those Maddogaritas. Next year we'll be #1 . . . somewhere.

It's our hope that this book goes beyond the battle for bragging rights for the "top bone in town" and stands instead as more a tribute to and visit with some of the pros, semi-pros, and backyard barons that make up the "mystique" of Kansas City BBQ.

Introduction

Grease, gristle, grime; several hazy, smoke-filled rooms; a crowded line huddled in the doorway, eagerly awaiting, and waiting, and waiting. A Depression-era soup kitchen? The first glance doesn't take in a pretty picture. But after closer inspection, the realization dawns — we have stumbled on barbecue heaven.

There are two types of decor at Kansas City barbecue restaurants, urban folksy and suburban casual. To the uninitiated, the first visit to a K.C. BBQ can be quite a surprise. The hype, excitement, and anticipation can be clouded by the first glimpse of linoleum-covered tables and the smoke-glazed windows of the order counter. Once the sleeves are rolled up, though, and that first juicy bone parts your lips, the earthy confines and hickory smoke seep into the bloodstream and you're hooked! Hooked on that wonderful habit, Kansas City barbecue.

It doesn't matter in what sort of restaurant atmosphere you indulge this passion. If it's a top-bone place and the food is great, there will be long lines, your hands will get covered with grease, sauce will ring your fingernails and lips, and your clothes will smell like smoke for at least a week. One doesn't just "eat" Kansas City barbecue — you have to live it, and more specifically you have to "live" several different BBQs until you find the one that matches your taste and personality. Once you've settled on the place you call *trés bone,* you'll argue to the death on the merits of your recipe of choice.

It shouldn't take a visitor long to get accustomed to Kansas City barbecue. Our town's pros have served up ribs, briskets, and hams for more notables than this volume will allow. Let's just say that more than one president has rolled down his sleeves and climbed back on Air Force One with a big old sauce eatin' grin on his face. More than one famous baseball player has been called out, lumbering around a curve ball, high and away, because his gullet was stuffed with ribs and beer. And more than one network personality has turned a one-hour layover at KCI into a five-hour feast at a favorite Kansas City barbecue bistro. It's not a sin to get all greased up on a lunch break or during a Saturday afternoon stroll. Just a word to the wise, though:

expect anything, go with the flow, and when in Kansas City, do as the Kansas Citians do — use a lot of napkins and send your clothes out to the cleaners the minute you get home.

The "How To" of Kansas City Barbecue

Kansas City is a barbecue Mecca. Other cities try to lay claim to great 'que; Memphis, Dallas, Houston, all are known for their own style of spice and cooking charm. But Kansas City has developed a unique reputation for fine barbecue restaurants and more importantly for fine "home cookers" of barbecue. A drive home from work will envelope you with the aromas billowing from backyard grills, the beckoning smell of hickory smoke in almost any neighborhood on almost any day of the year. Kansas Citians love to cook out. High winds, rain, or snow dampen neither the spirits nor the charcoal of a faithful backyard barbecue baron.

There are several types of outdoor cooking that seem to have been lumped into the category of "barbecue." When you get home from work and you throw a steak on the backyard cooker, some call this barbecuing. Let's set the record straight — the aforementioned act is *grilling*. When you cook anything outside for a period of less than one hour, this is, again, *grilling*. When we cook a chicken, brisket, or other larger piece of meat, it will take a little longer, we'll use a lot cooler fire, and the sweet smell of smoke will penetrate the meat. This, class, is *barbecue*.

There are many types of cookers on the market today. The most popular are the small hibachi, the Weber-type kettle, and the Hasty-Bake oven. You can grill on any of these, but a small hibachi produces too much heat to barbecue. A covered grill such as a kettle or charcoal oven will give you the most control over heat and smoke, and thus allow you to barbecue like a pro.

Once you've chosen a cooker, you need to learn how to build a fire. Some folks use starter fluid, but this can leave an unpleasant aroma that can spoil the meat; you can use newspaper to build the fire instead. Set the paper under the coals or use a metal cylinder charcoal starter chimney. Once the fire has been started, you want to keep adding coals to it, a few at a time. The idea is to keep a low, steady fire burning. The smoke will come from seasoned woods, not the blaze of grease from a raging hot fire.

A well-seasoned wood can "make" your barbecue; you can use one in particular or even mix several kinds to give a personal trademark to your barbecue fire. Hickory is the most commonly used wood and is recognized for its heavy smoke flavor. It's good for larger cuts of meat that cook over a low flame for a long time. Try hickory with turkey, brisket, pork loin, or whole hog. Mesquite is a hardwood that creates a hot fire, great for grilling steaks, chicken, and chops. Fruit woods, such as apple or cherry, produce a less harsh smoke and are good for fish and poultry. Whatever wood you choose, soak it in water for at least 30 minutes before burning. Add it slowly, as you do the charcoal, keeping the fire burning steady and slow. The wet wood not only burns slowly, but the water also adds moisture to the meat, helping to create a little professional magic in your cooker.

A pan of water placed in your smoker also helps to increase the humidity and allow the smoke to permeate the meat. The water keeps the meat juicy. In a covered smoker, place the meat off to one side, opposite the fire, with a pan of water opposite the meat and above the fire. This "indirect" method of cooking produces a flavor you'll treasure.

When you barbecue, keep in mind the time element and the amount of people you are cooking for. For example, if you want to cook ribs and chicken for 200 people on the Fourth of July, start the fire around midnight and it will be hot enough to start the ribs at around 1 a.m. For a crowd this size, you'll be cooking 50-60 slabs of ribs that will need to be moved every 45 minutes. The chicken goes in the cooker by afternoon, about two hours before serving time. By contrast, when you cook two slabs of ribs for the family, you can put them on around noon and eat at 5 p.m. (chicken will still take a couple of hours to cook). The idea in both scenarios is the same: cook for a long time on low heat with lots of smoke to season the meat.

In order to achieve the "perfect" barbecue, you need to buy your meat in the right place (that is, not just right out of the case at the supermarket) and you need to know what you're buying. For ribs, be sure to ask for pork spare ribs, 2½ pounds and down. The smaller the slab, the smaller the pig and the more tender the meat. For a great steaks, ask for the K.C. strip, 12 ounces each from the center cut. Get "choice" or better — what a cut! When buying chicken, get split breasts, and for pork chops, be sure to ask for extra thick. If you've decided to cook brisket, it's important to ask for the "flats" of a brisket; the butcher will remove most of the fat, and you'll get the most for your money.

There are some other secrets you need to know in order to cook like a pro. You need to season the meat before you cook it. You can use a liquid marinade or a dry rub. Ribs, briskets, steak, or chicken, any meat you choose will give a better presentation when it has been marinated beforehand. Many of the recipes that follow in this book will tell you how to coax that extra flavor from your barbecue.

To be quite honest, the best barbecue in Kansas City is cooked at home, my home. I'll eat at almost any barbecue restaurant, but I still think my cooking is the best. This sentiment is most evident at a barbecue contest. There are many of these, from spring throughout the summer, with the American Royal Contest ending the season in the fall. Once you've mastered the art of backyard 'que, you might want to take in a contest or two to learn a few more tricks of the trade. Kansas City is known for its world-renowned chefs in the barbecue tradition, and these titans win most of their awards at contests in this area.

The pages that follow will introduce you to several of Kansas City's masters of the barbecue art. Their recipes are simple to follow and will have you cooking like a pro in just a few weekends over the grill. So get the charcoal out and dig in. Kansas City barbecue can be yours at home.

Paul Kirk, C.E.C.
BARON OF BARBECUE

Paul Kirk is a celebrity chef in Kansas City and is known throughout America's barbecue belt and beyond as a championship pitmaster. Chef Paul has won over 200 awards in local, national, and international competitions. A frequent guest on radio and television talk shows, he also has been featured and quoted in the *Kansas City Times,* the *Kansas City Star,* the *Tacoma News Tribune,* the *Goat Gap Gazette,* and the *Portland Oregonian.* In addition, his recipes are included in two new best-selling books: *The Passion of Barbeque* (1988, Pig Out Publications) and *The All-American Guide to Authentic Barbecuing* (1988, Harcourt). Chef Paul is a charter judge and the official pitmaster of the American Royal National Barbecue Sauce Contest. He is also the executive chef at Trinity Lutheran Hospital in Kansas City and is known around the country as the Kansas City Baron of Barbecue.

One year at the Great Lenexa Barbecue Battle Paul won "Best BBQ Atmosphere." He comments on this by saying, "My place was trashy. One table had a tablecloth and another didn't, but I won because anybody that came by that wanted to talk barbecue was talked to by me . . . I love to talk barbecue!" His tips on making the best ribs are to use a rub seasoning, cook over a slow indirect fire, and try a combination of oak, hickory, and apple woods.

Chef Paul is currently writing a recipe exchange column for the *Goat Gap Gazette* and for the Kansas City Barbeque Society *Bull Sheet.*

Barbecued Whole Hog

75-85 lb. hog
olive or vegetable oil
salt and pepper to taste
apple (optional)
2 gal. barbecue baste

Assuming you have a smoker big enough to cook a hog, allow 2 weeks to a month lead time with your butcher. Gather plenty of wood and charcoal.

Wash the hog inside and out. Trim away any loose skin or fat. Remove the kidneys. Pry the mouth open and insert a short log (to be replaced with the apple later on). Start with the fire at about 350 degrees. While it's burning down, rub hog with oil inside and out. Then rub the cavity with salt and pepper. Find the tenderloin (in the inside, from the rear end to about the middle of the pig) and cover with aluminum foil; hold foil in place with toothpicks. Then wrap the ears, feet, and snout in foil.

Place the hog in the smoker with the front end close to the heat. Smoke this way for 5 to 6 hours or until the shoulders reach an internal temperature of 90-100 degrees. Turn the hog and mop generously with baste. Check the temperature often. When the hams reach 110-120 degrees, remove the foil so the ears and snout will brown. Pork is done when the internal temperature reaches 165 degrees; it should take 12-15 hours to cook thoroughly. Be concerned about undercooking rather than overcooking.

Serves 50-75

Barbecued Pork Burgers

2 lbs. ground pork
1/4 C. buttermilk
2 t. seasoned salt
1 t. black pepper
1/4 t. garlic powder
1/4 t. ground oregano
1/4 C. minced onion

Combine all ingredients. Mix thoroughly and form into 1/4- pound patties.

Sear patties on the grill, then reduce flame and cook over direct heat for about 10 minutes on each side.

Serves 4-6

The Baron's Barbecue Chicken

2 whole chicken fryers, cut in half
2 T. garlic salt
1 T. paprika
1 T. black pepper

BASTE

1 C. water	2 T. instant onions
1 C. catsup	3 T. Worcestershire sauce
1/4 C. cider vinegar	1 t. dry mustard

Mix garlic salt, paprika, and pepper. Sprinkle over the chicken, covering the entire surface. Place the chicken on the grill skin-side up over a medium-hot fire. Cover and grill for 30 minutes; turn and cook another 15 minutes.

While the chicken is grilling, make the baste by stirring the ingredients together in a small saucepan. Bring mixture to a boil, then turn down heat and simmer for 10 minutes.

When the chicken is tender, baste the entire surface and cook for another 5 minutes; turn and baste again. Chicken is done when it has a good glaze on it (be careful not to burn).

Serves 4-6

Barbecued Rib Roast

7 lb. boneless rib roast
lemon pepper

MARINADE

3 1/2 C. water
1 1/2 C. burgundy
1/2 C. red wine vinegar
1 medium onion, sliced thin

4 stalks celery, diced
2 cloves garlic, pressed
2 bay leaves, crushed

Combine marinade ingredients in a pan and sauté until browned. Rub lemon pepper generously over roast, then place meat and marinade mixture in a large sealable plastic bag. Marinate in the refrigerator for 4 hours.

Prepare fire on one side of grill. Remove roast from bag and place at opposite end of grill from the fire. Cover and cook at 150 degrees using indirect heat, 2 1/2 hours or 25 minutes per pound. Add moistened hickory chunks to the fire periodically.

Serves 14-20

The Baron's Steak Sauce

1/2 lb. beef suet (fat trimmings from brisket or steak)
1/4 lb. butter
1 C. fresh mushrooms, sliced thin
1 clove garlic, minced
1/2 C. dry white wine
2 T. A-1 steak sauce
1 T. Worcestershire sauce

Place suet in a large skillet and heat until 1/4 cup of grease is rendered. Remove any remaining suet and add butter, mushrooms, and garlic. Cook until mushrooms are done. Add remaining ingredients and stir. Reduce heat and simmer for 15 minutes or until mixture starts to thicken. Serve over steaks or to the side.

Yields about 3 1/2 cups

Guy Simpson
K.C. RIB DOCTOR

The road to a barbecue feature article in the March 1987 issue of *Woman's Day* was paved with many bags of charcoal for the K.C. Rib Doctor, Guy Simpson. A "lark" that ended with a Kansas State championship in ribs has brought barbecue success and fame to Guy. The Rib Doctor developed a rib rub that earned him third place in the Diddy-Wa-Diddy Sauce Contest, a product that has been featured in the Kansas display at Bloomingdale's in New York. A veteran of many barbecue contests, the Rib Doctor is the prime example of a backyard baron who has parlayed his skill into the pro ranks of the barbecue elite. His special talent is responsible for a very successful catering business that will barbecue on site for groups from 50 to 2,000. The Rib Doctor is a charter member of the Kansas City Barbeque Society and has served on the board of directors for the last two years.

At a barbecue contest, you'll find Guy at the helm of the "Silver Bullet," an eight-foot, insulated, stainless steel cooking machine on wheels. Also distinctively, he wears a $10,000.00 hat; that is, each pin on the hat represents a cooking contest, which in turn represents a monetary expenditure. With each contest, his hat gets more expensive. Guy's advice on seasoning ribs with his Rib Doctor Dry Seasoning is to "powder them like you would a baby's bottom!"

Guy's Chicken Wings

1 lb. chicken wings

MARINADE

5 T. soy sauce
5 T. lemon juice
1 T. honey
2 T. catsup
5 T. Rib Doctor Dry Seasoning

Divide each wing into two parts at the joint. Mix marinade ingredients in a bowl, then add wings and coat well. Marinate for 2 hours.

Cook wings over prepared coals 15 minutes, then turn and brush on remaining marinade. Continue cooking for 15 minutes. Due to the honey coating, watch wings closely to avoid burning.

Serves 4

Chinese Pork Loin

2 lbs. pork tenderloin
5 T. rum
5 T. light soy sauce
4 T. Rib Doctor Dry Seasoning

Combine seasoning ingredients and rub into meat. Let stand for 2 hours before cooking. Barbecue slowly for about 1 hour. When meat has cooled, cut into thin slices.

Serves 6

Quick Grilled Pork Steaks

4 pork steaks (1/2 in. thick)
4 T. Rib Doctor Dry Seasoning
barbecue sauce

Cover both sides of the meat lightly with seasoning. Grill at a distance of 5 inches from moderate coals for 40 minutes, turning often. Apply your favorite barbecue sauce and cook for 10 more minutes, turning often to avoid burning.

Serves 4

Trout in a Basket

4 whole trout
1/2 C. all-purpose flour
4 t. Rib Doctor Dry Seasoning
1/4 C. butter, melted
lemon wedges

Gut trout; remove skin and heads. In a bowl, combine flour and spices. Dip fish in seasoned flour, coating well, and place in a well-greased wire basket. Grill over hot coals about 10 minutes. Turn and baste with butter. Grill until fish flakes easily, about 10 more minutes. Baste often with butter. Serve with lemon wedges.

Trout can be placed directly on the grill, but use caution when turning.

Serves 4-6

Spicy Eye of Round Steak

3 lbs. beef eye of round steak
1 bottle Italian dressing
4 T. Rib Doctor Dry Seasoning
1 small jar German-style mustard

Marinate meat overnight in Italian dressing, using a sealable plastic bag or covered bowl, and refrigerate.

Rub dry seasoning on the meat, then cover with a thin coat of mustard. Place meat on a roasting rack in the center of the grill. Use a drip pan under meat to avoid flames. Cook until meat thermometer registers 140 degrees, or about 1 hour. Let stand for 10 minutes before carving, then slice thin.

Serves 6-8

Fuzzy Navel Steak

1 sirloin steak (1 in. thick)

MARINADE

3/4 C. fresh orange juice (2 oranges)
1/4 C. light soy sauce
1 clove garlic, minced
1/4 t. ground clove
4 T. Rib Doctor Dry Seasoning

Combine ingredients to make the marinade. Place steak in a sealable plastic bag with marinade and refrigerate for 2-4 hours. Turn often.

Grill to your desired taste.

Serves 1-2

"Poor Man" Steak

1 round steak (2 in. thick)

MARINADE

1/2 C. light soy sauce
5 T. honey
1/4 C. cider vinegar
1 1/2 C. Italian dressing
2 green onions, chopped fine (tops included)
1 T. ground ginger
4 T. Rib Doctor Dry Seasoning

Blend all marinade ingredients and cover. Trim steak and marinate for 4 hours at room temperature, turning meat every hour.

Grill steak for 8 minutes over prepared coals, then turn and baste with marinade for 4 minutes. Repeat this process, turning and basting two more times for a total cooking time of 20 minutes, which will produce a perfect medium steak. Let meat stand for 10 minutes and then slice as thin as possible, diagonally across the grain.

Serves 8

Karen Putman, C.E.C.
FLOWER OF THE FLAMES

From Michael Jackson to the Final Four, Karen Putman's barbecue is world famous. She is the executive chef for the Eddy's catering organization and has received many awards for her various cooking styles. She began barbecuing at the 1984 American Royal Barbecue Contest and has since won over 100 local, state, national, and international cooking awards, including the Kansas State Professional Championships in 1986 and 1988. Karen has served as many as 20,000 people at once, but prefers to join with her family and friends and cook at barbecue contests. Her goal is to win the National Barbecue Championship, and to her credit she just might.

Karen's approach to barbecue can best be summarized as "gourmet." Her traditional sauces range from mild to hot and sassy, and she has also produced and bottled a raspberry barbecue sauce called "Flower of the Flames," a nickname dubbed her by Remus Powers, founder of the Diddy-Wa-Diddy Sauce Contest. For the health conscious, her "Very Low Salt and Sugar-free Barbecue Sauce" should also be a hit.

Smoked Chicken Salad

6 chicken breasts
Flower of the Flames Raspberry
  Barbecue Sauce
torn lettuce, spinach, romaine,
  and endive

6 hard-boiled eggs, quartered
6 tomatoes, quartered

DRESSING

1 bottle Flower of the Flames
  Raspberry Barbecue Sauce

6 T. olive oil
8 T. raspberry vinegar

Marinate the chicken breasts in barbecue sauce overnight in the refrigerator, then cook chicken in a smoker for 2 hours at 225 degrees.

Slice smoked breasts and place in the center of the mixed greens, surrounded by the quartered eggs and tomatoes. Serve with raspberry dressing on the side.

Serves 6-8

Smoked Sausage Stuffed Duck

4-5 lb. domestic duckling
salt

STUFFING

1/4 lb. smoked sausage (1/2 in. cubes)
1/2 C. finely chopped celery
1/2 C. finely chopped apple
1/4 C. finely chopped onion

1/4 t. ground red pepper
2 T. butter or margarine
4 C. plain croutons
1/4 C. chicken broth

In a medium saucepan, cook sausage, celery, apple, onion, and pepper in butter until vegetables are tender. Remove from heat. Place croutons in large mixing bowl. Sprinkle with sausage mixture and chicken broth. Toss lightly until well mixed, then set aside.

Rinse duck and pat dry with paper towels. Sprinkle inside cavity with salt. Spoon some of the stuffing into the neck cavity. Fasten the neck skin securely to the back of the bird with a small skewer. Lightly spoon remaining stuffing into the body. Tie legs securely to the tail. Twist wing tips under back. Prick skin all over with a fork. Smoke 4-5 hours.

Serves 6-10

Marinated Smoked Flank Steak

3-5 lbs. flank steak

MARINADE

1 qt. Coca-Cola
2 C. oil
2 C. vinegar

6 cloves garlic
salt and pepper to taste

Prepare marinade and marinate meat in refrigerator overnight. Remove steak from marinade and smoke at 200 degrees for 6-8 hours, basting every 20-30 minutes with remaining marinade.

Serves 6-8

Smoked Stuffed Veal

8 lbs. veal, pounded to 1 in. thick
1 lb. ground veal
4 oz. pork fat
4 eggs
3 oz. fresh bread crumbs
16 oz. spinach, blanched,
    drained, and chopped
3 T. chopped parsley
4 oz. blanched dried apple,
    chopped

40 pitted dates
4 oz. onion, chopped
4 oz. bacon, diced
2 cloves garlic, minced
1/2 C. chopped green onions
1/2 t. basil
1/2 t. marjoram
1/2 t. rosemary
salt and pepper to taste

Using the fine blade in a meat grinder, grind together ground veal and pork fat several times. Chill. Combine eggs, bread crumbs, spinach, parsley, dates, and apples and add to ground veal mixture.

Sauté onion, bacon, garlic, and green onions until vegetables are tender and bacon crisp. Mix basil, marjoram, rosemary, salt, and pepper and add to bacon mixture. Chill, then add to ground veal mixture. Stuff meat by spreading veal mixture over pounded veal. Roll up, wrap in bacon slices, and smoke for 4 hours.

Serves 12-16

Smoked Stuffed Leg of Lamb

6-7 lb. leg of lamb (about 4 lbs. after boning and trim)
2 large bunches spinach
3 T. olive oil
2 large cloves garlic, minced
1/2 C. fresh bread crumbs
1/4 C. raisins
1/4 C. pine nuts
1/4 C. fresh chopped basil
2 oz. cream cheese
1/2 t. salt
1/4 t. freshly ground black pepper

Bone, trim, and butterfly leg of lamb. Wash spinach leaves and remove stems; dry with paper towels. Stack 10-12 leaves on top of each other, then roll lengthwise, jellyroll style. Cut crosswise into 1/8-inch shreds. Repeat with remaining leaves. In a medium skillet, heat olive oil over high heat; stir in spinach and garlic. Tossing and stirring often, cook for 2 minutes or until most of the liquid has evaporated.

Spoon spinach mixture into a medium bowl and stir in bread crumbs, raisins, pine nuts, basil, cheese, salt, and pepper. Spread lamb with spinach mixture and roll up, jellyroll style, beginning from the long side. With a heavy string, tie rolled lamb at 1-inch intervals. Smoke for 5-6 hours.

Serves 6-8

Dan Morey
CHEF DAN

Chef Dan Morey, from McCune, Kansas, has seen more sheep shearin' and goat ropin' than most of us have ever dreamed of. He still wears his cowboy boots and straw hat, but he's traded in his rope for a pair of barbecue tongs. Dan is a charter member of the Kansas City Barbeque Society and his barbecue prowess has brought him countless awards and acclaim, including a People's Choice Award for one of the top five mild barbecue sauces in the United States. Chef Dan's barbecue sauce was the most award-winning Kansas City sauce in 1988 according to the organizers of the American Royal Diddy-Wa-Diddy Sauce Contest and is a mainstay in his native McCune, where it's always available for sale at City Hall, Maxine's Beauty Parlor, and the Farmers' Co-op.

Dan is a member of the American Culinary Federation and is chef and production manager of food services at St. Luke's Hospital in Kansas City. He offers the following advice on barbecuing: "I use mulberry wood and cook slowly. Baste frequently with a salt-free baste, because salt pulls moisture out of meat."

Chef Dan's Leg of Lamb

5-6 lb. boneless leg of lamb
olive oil
garlic, minced
rosemary, fresh, chopped
salt
pepper
1 lb. Italian sausage links
roasting twine

Remove netting from around the meat and unroll the roast. Coat all surfaces with olive oil, then rub with garlic, rosemary, salt, and pepper. Place the Italian sausage where the bone would have been in the leg, roll the leg up, and tie with roasting twine.

Smoke for 10 hours at 200 degrees or until desired doneness (be sure the sausage is thoroughly cooked before eating).

Serves 8-10

Smoked Brisket, K.C. Style

12-14 lbs. brisket, untrimmed
olive oil
1/4 C. cayenne pepper
1/2 C. paprika
1/4 C. pepper

Make a dry rub with the spices and set aside. Rub brisket with olive oil followed by dry rub.

Smoke meat for 15 hours at 180-200 degrees. Remove from the smoker, wrap in plastic wrap, then cover completely with aluminum foil. Return brisket to the smoker for 5 more hours at 180-200 degrees. Remove from smoker and let stand for 10 minutes, then slice thinly.

Serves 6-10

Perfect Wild Game

4-5 lbs. favorite game (rabbit, duck, goose, or pheasant)

MARINADE

2 C. distilled vinegar
1 t. thyme leaves
1 T. black pepper
1 t. cayenne pepper
1 t. curry powder
1 T. garlic powder
1 T. onion powder

Combine marinade ingredients in a bowl and set aside. Clean game thoroughly. Place meat in a sealable plastic bag with marinade and marinate overnight.

Place on a rotisserie or split and broil over medium hot coals. Baste often with remaining marinade until done.

Serves 4-6

Rich Davis
BBQ ENTREPRENEUR

Rich Davis, a well-known barbecue figure and the creator of K.C. Masterpiece sauce, was introduced to the all-American art of backyard barbecue by his father while growing up in Joplin, Missouri, and Topeka, Kansas. By 1977, what had been a most enjoyable hobby beckoned to him professionally—he decided to start selling "the best sauce he had ever made." In fact, he gave up his practice as a family and child psychiatrist to immerse himself in the pursuit of barbecue excellence.

Dr. Davis keeps his seasoned hand in many barbecue-related projects. He has co-authored *All About Barbecue Kansas City Style* and *The All-American Barbecue Book* with Shifra Stein, and he narrates the only videocassette available on the topic, "The Secrets, Sauces and Savvy of American Barbecue and Grilling." Rich has appeared on national television and has written food articles for *Ladies Home Journal* and *Playboy* magazine. If you watch the movie credits, you'll also see that he was the "technical barbecue consultant" on the set of "Murphy's Romance."

With the opening of a K.C. Masterpiece Barbecue & Grill restaurant in suburban Kansas City and then more recently one in St. Louis, Rich and his sons, Charles and Rich II, have scored another success. His favorite barbecue rule is short and sweet: "Cook it low and smoke it slow."

Barbequed Whole Tenderloin

3 large pork tenderloins (or 1 whole beef tenderloin, trimmed)

MARINADE

1 C. soy sauce
1/3 C. toasted oriental sesame oil
3 large cloves garlic, minced

1 T. ground ginger
1 t. MSG (optional)

SAUCE

19 oz. K.C. Masterpiece sauce
1/3 C. soy sauce

1/4 C. toasted oriental sesame oil
1 large clove garlic, finely minced

Bring meat to room temperature. In a small bowl, mix together marinade ingredients. Pour marinade over meat in a glass or enameled pan (or use a sealable plastic bag). Cover and marinate overnight in the refrigerator.

Place tenderloins over a low fire on a charcoal grill (with moistened hickory added to smoke). Barbecue with lid closed, turning every 15 minutes and basting with marinade, for approximately 11 hours (for pork) or until done to taste (for beef).

Serves 6-8

K.C. Masterpiece
Barbequed Baked Beans

2 (16 oz.) cans pork and beans, drained
3/4 C. K.C. Masterpiece Original sauce
1 oz. golden raisins
1/2 C. brown sugar
1 tart apple (such as Jonathan), peeled, cored, and chopped
1 medium onion, chopped
3 strips uncooked bacon, cut in half
    (or substitute 2 T. butter or margarine)

Preheat oven to 350 degrees. Mix all ingredients except bacon in a 2-quart baking dish. Top with uncooked bacon (or butter). Bake uncovered for 1 hour.

Serves 6-8

Barbequed Stuffed Cabbage Rolls

3 lbs. lean ground beef
1 1/2 t. salt
1 t. cracked black pepper
1 T. minced garlic
1/2 C. cooked rice
2 T. Worcestershire sauce
1/2 C. chopped green bell pepper
1 (12 oz.) can Ro-Tel tomatoes and chilies, drained and chopped
3 C. chopped onion
2 eggs, lightly beaten
1/2 C. crushed plain soda crackers
2 or 3 heads fresh cabbage (enough to yield 36 large leaves)
3 1/2 C. K.C. Masterpiece Original sauce

In a large bowl, mix together by hand the ground beef, rice, Worcestershire sauce, green peppers, tomatoes and chilies, 1 cup of the onion, and the eggs and crackers. Cut out and discard the hard center of the cabbages. Place cabbages in a large kettle and pour boiling water over to cover. Simmer over low heat until leaves can be easily removed, about 7 or 8 minutes.

Preheat oven to 350 degrees. Roll the meat mixture by hand into sausage-like shapes, about 3 inches long and 1 inch thick. Place each meat roll on a cabbage leaf and fold leaf over the stuffing, tucking in the ends to seal. Thoroughly grease two 9 x 13-inch oblong baking dishes. Spread the remaining chopped onion over the bottom of each dish, then top with rows of cabbage rolls, seam side down. Pour 3 cups of the barbecue sauce evenly over the rolls and cover pan tightly with aluminum foil. Bake for 1 hour. Remove foil and baste the rolls with pan juices. Uncover and bake for an additional 15 minutes. Serve with the remaining barbecue sauce spooned over the rolls.

Serves 12-15

Coleslaw with Boiled Dressing

1/2 t. celery salt
1/4 t. garlic salt
1 t. dry mustard
1/8 t. ground black pepper
1/4 t. salt
1/4 t. paprika
2 T. sugar
1/2 C. water
1 egg
1/3 C. cider vinegar
4 C. shredded cabbage

Dissolve celery salt, garlic salt, dry mustard, pepper, salt, paprika, and sugar in the water. Set aside. Beat the egg lightly in a small, heavy saucepan. Place over low heat and immediately beat in the vinegar and dissolved spice mixture, stirring constantly until the mixture thickens (about 5 minutes.) Chill. Pour over shredded cabbage and toss well.

Serves 3-4

Hasty-Bake
OVEN MANUFACTURER

The Hasty-Bake charcoal oven manufacturing company has built their 40-year-old business on a simple barbecue principle: controlled heat produces quality meat. In this case, the "controlled heat" is obtained through the use of six different regulators.

A Hasty-Bake oven's *lift mechanism* allows the firebox to travel vertically, from a lowest position that produces a 100-200 degree environment (suitable for smoking) to its highest position, which generates searing heat. The *heat deflector* creates a baffling effect that protects the meat from direct flame, which in turn ensures that moisture is retained. The *grease drain* system also helps to control heat. By channeling grease to an outside container, both grease smoke and flare-ups are eliminated.

An interesting feature of Hasty-Bake ovens is how they retain heat. There are no vents in the oven hood; they're below the meat, where the smoke must pass through the food twice, once up and then back down again as it is pushed out by the additional heat and smoke that is being produced.

The diagram on the following page identifies these various elements of the Hasty-Bake ovens.

How the Hasty-Bake oven works:

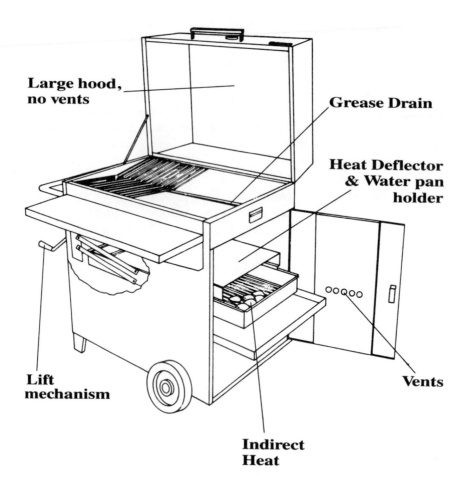

Large hood, no vents

Grease Drain

Heat Deflector & Water pan holder

Lift mechanism

Vents

Indirect Heat

Chad's "Baby Back" Ribs

2-3 slabs baby back pork ribs
seasoned salt
1/2 C. soy sauce
1/2 C. Worcestershire sauce
1/2 T. minced onion per slab
1/2 T. minced garlic per slab
1/2 T. coarse ground pepper per slab

Sprinkle meat side of thawed ribs with seasoned salt. Hand pack into meat, then baste with soy and Worcestershire sauce. Sprinkle on onion, garlic, and pepper and baste again.

Cook, bone side down, until meat begins to pull away from bone, not less than 2 hours and not more than 3 1/2 hours. Baste every 30 minutes and smoke generously with hickory wood. (Firebox should be at "2/3 down" position with heat deflector in place.)

Serves 4-6

Simmons's Smoked Salmon

7-10 lb. salmon, cleaned and dressed
1/4 C. soy sauce
1/4 C. Worcestershire sauce
1 t. minced garlic
1/4 C. light margarine, melted
1/2 C. white wine

Place salmon lengthwise on the back side of the grill, resting on top of heavy-duty aluminum foil. Combine soy sauce and Worcestershire sauce and use to baste fish. Sprinkle on garlic. Mix margarine and white wine and pour directly on fish.

Maintaining low heat with firebox in the lower position, cook for approximately 1 hour and turn; skin should stick and pull away from body of fish. Cook for approximately 30 minutes more, for a total of 1 1/2 hours. Use a spatula to separate the halves and lift out the bones before serving the fish.

Serves 6-8

Scott's S-m-o-o-t-h Orange Roughy

2 orange roughy fillets
1/2 C. milk
2 T. butter
lemon slices
1 whole lemon, halved
1/2 cup diced green pepper
1/2 cup diced red pepper
1/2 cup sliced mushrooms
purple onion rings, thinly sliced

Soak fish in milk for 15 minutes per side; remove and dry with a paper towel. Melt butter in baster pan, then lay enough lemon slices in the bottom of the pan to support the fillets. Lay fish over lemon slices and squeeze 1/2 lemon over each fillet. Cover with green and red peppers, mushrooms, additional lemon slices, and onion rings.

Let stand for 1 hour in the refrigerator, then cook over medium deflected heat for 30 minutes.

Serves 2

Deb's Lip-Lickin' Chicken

4 chicken breasts
seasoned salt to taste
lemon pepper to taste
coarse ground pepper to taste
minced garlic to taste
1/2 C. soy sauce
1/2 C. Worcestershire sauce

Wash chicken breasts and pat dry. Rub with spices and place on the grill, meat-side down, searing for 5 minutes. Flip to bone-side down and sear for 5 more minutes. Lower firebox to 2/3 down position and, with heat deflector in place, cook for 1 hour and 15 minutes.

Put soy sauce and Worcestershire in a spray bottle and use to baste meat frequently (every 20 minutes).

Serves 4-6

The "Where To" of Kansas City Barbecue

Up to this point you've gotten a little history, a few pointers, and some of the most mouth-watering recipes for barbecue in the world. Now it's time for a field trip.

In order to give this book some credibility and to make some use of my statistics and marketing research background, I put together a short survey on barbecue. After tallying several hundred responses to this questionnaire, the answers proved to be a reaffirmation of my major thesis — there are just as many good places for barbecue as there are people to pick them.

However, the survey did tell me that people in a mass will agree on several issues. The following pages offer lists of the "Top 12" restaurants in several categories of barbecue that the survey produced, as well as a "directory" of the 38 barbecue restaurants that received at least one vote in the survey. Immediately preceding these results a sample completed survey has been reproduced.

One final caveat: the restaurants are not listed within the categories in any sort of order of preference; it's all *strictly* alphabetical. You can be your own judge after getting in the car and trying the bounty of several of these places. Happy trails.

Here's a sample completed survey:

Where would you send an out of town guest to eat K.C. B.B.Q.?

Greasehouse + low budget 1. Bryant's

UPSCALE 2. Rosedale

3. Masterpiece

Moderate $ -Tavern Ambiance 4. Jake Edwards

What B.B.Q. Restaurant serves the best? 5. Bodee's

Ribs _Bodee's_

Brisket/beef Sandwiches ① Bryant's, ② Masterpiece, ③ Bodee's

Ham Sandwiches N/A "It ain't Barbecue!"

Chicken BBQ: Bryant's ; Grilled : Masterpiece

B.B.Q. Sauce ① Bryant's, ② Masterpiece, ③ Bodee's

Beans _Master piece_

Other (name item) _Burnt Ends_ _Keegan's_

THE ⊙BEST⊙ OVERALL BEST: Bodee's + Masterpiece
BBQ RESTUARANT

My Standard of (BEST) is:

1) Quality of food
2) Quantity of food
3) Price / Value
4) Variety

Keegan's Coleslaw: + Lil Jake's

by Ardie A. Davis
founder of the

Diddy Wa Diddy Sauce Contest !!

Results of Venable's 1989 Barbecue Survey

The restaurants appear in alphabetical order:

BEST RIBS IN TOWN

Arrowhead Stadium
Arthur Bryant Barbecue
Bodee's Bar-B-Que
Gates & Son's Bar-B-Q
Hayward's Pit Bar-B-Que
K.C. Masterpiece Barbecue
  & Grill
Keegan's Bar-B-Q
Marty's BBQ
Rosedale Barbecue
Smoke Stack Bar-B-Q
Wyandot Barbeque
Zarda Bar-B-Q

BEST BEEF IN TOWN

Arthur Bryant Barbecue
Bodee's Bar-B-Que
Gates & Son's Bar-B-Q
Hayward's Pit Bar-B-Que
Jake Edwards Bar-B-Q
K.C. Masterpiece Barbecue
  & Grill
Li'l Jake's
Marty's BBQ
Rosedale Barbecue
Smoke Stack Bar-B-Q
Wyandot Barbeque
Zarda Bar-B-Q

BEST HAM IN TOWN

Arthur Bryant Barbecue
Bodee's Bar-B-Que
Gates & Son's Bar-B-Q
Hayward's Pit Bar-B-Que
Hunter's Smokehouse
K.C. Masterpiece Barbecue
  & Grill
Keegan's Bar-B-Q
Marty's BBQ
Oscar's Bar-B-Q
Rosedale Barbecue
Wyandot Barbecue
Zarda Bar-B-Q

BEST CHICKEN IN TOWN

Arrowhead Stadium
Arthur Bryant Barbecue
Boyd & Son's Barbecue
Gates & Son's Bar-B-Q
Hayward's Pit Bar-B-Que
Jake Edwards Bar-B-Q
Joe's Restaurant and Bar-B-Q
K.C. Masterpiece Barbecue
  & Grill
Rosedale Barbecue
Smoke Stack Bar-B-Q
Wyandot Barbecue
Zarda Bar-B-Q

Barbecue Survey

BEST BEANS IN TOWN

Bodee's Bar-B-Que
Gates & Son's Bar-B-Q
Hayward's Pit Bar-B-Que
Hunter's Smokehouse
Jake Edwards Bar-B-Q
K.C. Masterpiece Barbecue
    & Grill
Marty's BBQ
Rosedale Barbecue
Smoke Stack Bar-B-Q
Winslow's City Market
    Smokehouse Barbecue
Wyandot Barbeque
Zarda Bar-B-Q

BEST SAUCE IN TOWN

Arthur Bryant Barbecue
Bodee's Bar-B-Que
Gates & Son's Bar-B-Q
Hayward's Pit Bar-B-Que
Jake Edwards Bar-B-Q
K.C. Masterpiece Barbecue
    & Grill
Quick's Seventh Street Bar-B-Q
Rosedale Barbecue
Smoke Stack Bar-B-Q
Snead's Bar-B-Q
Wyandot Barbecue
Zarda Bar-B-Q

THE TOP BBQS IN TOWN

Arthur Bryant Barbecue
Bodee's Bar-B-Que
Gates & Son's Bar-B-Q
Hayward's Pit Bar-B-Que
Hunter's Smokehouse
K.C. Masterpiece Barbecue
    & Grill

Rosedale Barbecue
Smoke Stack Bar-B-Q
Wyandot Barbeque
Zarda Bar-B-Q
Jake Edwards Bar-B-Q
Marty's BBQ

Directory of Barbecue Restaurants

M any of the following restaurants offer carry out and catering as well as eating in. Check with them for individual services. The asterisk (*) identifies the "Top 12" restaurants from the survey, which are also featured on the map inside the front cover.

Arrowhead Stadium
1 Arrowhead Drive
921-2225

*Arthur Bryant Barbecue
1727 Brooklyn
231-1123

Bates City BBQ
313 Market Street
Bates City, MO
625-4961

Bobby Bell's Bar-B-Que
7013 N. Oak Trafficway
436-2917

*Bodee's Bar-B-Que
5620 E. Bannister Road
966-0503
9501 Quivira Road
492-0503

Boyd & Sons Barbecue
5510 Prospect Avenue
523-0436

The Depot
2702 Bell Street
Avondale, MO
452-2100

*Gates & Son's Bar-B-Q
4707 The Paseo
923-0900

1411 Swope Parkway
921-0409

2001 W. 103rd Terrace
383-1752

1026 State Avenue
621-1134

1221 Brooklyn Avenue
483-3880

10440 E. Highway 40
353-5880

Guy & Mae's
119 W. Williams Street
Williamsburg, KS
913/746-8830

43

*Hayward's Pit Bar-B-Que
11051 Antioch Road
451-8080

Hickory Stick Pit Bar-B-Que
10223 W. 75th Street
631-5133

Houston's
4640 Wornall Road
561-8542
7111 W. 95th Street
642-0630

*Hunter's Smokehouse
9600 Antioch Road
649-3002

*Jake Edwards Bar-B-Q
5107 Main Street
531-8878

Joe's Restaurant and Bar-B-Q
7907 State Line Road
523-1950

Johnny's Hickory House Bar-B-Q
5959 Broadmoor Drive
432-0777

*K.C. Masterpiece Barbecue & Grill
10985 Metcalf Avenue
345-1199

Keegan's Bar-B-Q
325 E. 135th Street
942-7550

Li'l Jake's
1227 Grand Avenue
283-0880

Main Street Inn
714 Main Street
761-9016

*Marty's BBQ
2516 N.E. Vivion Road
453-2222

Richard France's K.C. BBQ
212 W. 9th Street
421-7675

Ricky's Pit Bar-B-Que
3801 Leavenworth Road
287-1010

*Rosedale Barbecue
632 Southwest Boulevard
262-0343

Santa Fe Trail Bar-B-Que
1404 E. Santa Fe Trail
782-7352

*Smoke Stack Bar-B-Q
13441 Holmes Road
(Martin City)
942-9141
8219 S. Highway 71
333-2011
430 W. 85th Street
444-5542

Snead's Barb-Q
171st Street & Holmes Road
331-9858

Sport's Restaurant
13905 Noland Court
461-8065

**Stephenson's Apple
Tree Inn**
5755 Northwood Road
587-9300
Old Apple Farm
E. Highway 40 at Lee's
Summit Road
373-5400

**Winslow's City Market
Smokehouse Barbecue**
20 E. 5th Street
471-7427

*Wyandot Barbeque
8441 State Avenue
788-7554

7215 W. 75th Street
341-0609

519-521 E. Santa Fe Trail
829-2249

11824 Blue Ridge Boulevard
765-1323

*Zarda Bar-B-Q
87th Street and Quivira Road
492-2330
214 N. Highway 7
229-9999

Books on Barbecue

A saucy sampling of additional reading pleasure!

The All-American Barbecue Book by Rich Davis and Shifra Stein (1988, Vintage Books)

Barbecue and Smoke Cookery by Maggie Waldren (1989, Ortho Publications)

Barbecue Greats — Memphis Style by Carolyn Wells (1989, Pig Out Publications)

Barbecuing, Grilling and Smoking by the California Culinary Academy (1988, Ortho Publications)

Great American Barbeque by "Smoky" Hale (1989, Abacus Publishing Company)

Grill Lovers Cookbook (1985, from Char-Broil, Columbus, GA)

The Joy of Grilling by Joe Famularo (1988, Barron's)

Memphis Barbecue, Barbeque, Bar-B-Que, Bar-B-Q, B-B-Q by Carolyn Wells (1989, Pig Out Publications)

Real Barbecue by Greg Johnson and Vince Staten (1988, Harper & Row)

Pig Out Publications
Order Form

ORDER DIRECT — CALL (816) 842-8880

YES! I want to start cooking like the pros. Send me:

_____ copy/copies of *Barbecue Greats-Memphis Style* for $12.95 plus $2 shipping.

_____ copy/copies of *Kansas City BBQ* for $9.95 plus $1 shipping.

_____ copy/copies of *Memphis Barbecue Barbeque Bar-B-Que Bar-B-Q B-B-Q for* $6.95 plus $1 shipping.

_____ copy/copies of *The Passion of Barbeque* for $9.95 plus $2 shipping.

METHOD OF PAYMENT:

Enclosed is my check for $ _____ , made payable to *Pig Out Publications*

Please charge to my credit card: _____ VISA _____ MasterCard

Account # _____ Exp. date _____

Signature _____

SHIP TO:

Name _____

Address _____

City _____ State _____

ZIP _____ Daytime phone _____

SEND AS A GIFT TO:

Name _____

Address _____

City _____ State _____

ZIP _____ Daytime phone _____

FROM: _____

Pig Out Publications   101 W. 18th Ave.   N. Kansas City, MO 64116